The Weight of Dreams

Jeevan Bhagwat

The Weight of Dreams
By Jeevan Bhagwat

The Weight of Dreams
ISBN: 978-0-9819797-6-2

IN PUBLICATIONS
14 Lorraine Circle, Waban, MA 02468

DEDICATION

For my Mother and Father

Who taught me the importance of love and dreams

INTRODUCTION

The Weight of Dreams is a journey
through the sensitive soulscape of unrequited love,
that universal sting in the hazardous
realm of Eros.

How much do dreams weigh?

They can be

"weightless as waterlilies"

or

"heavy on the chest."

The heart of the poet reflects the beauty and caprice of Nature,
the drama of shifting sky and changing seasons,
love's powerful metaphors.

This moving collection reveals a poignant self-honesty and
a rare tenderness,
the essence of the poet's appeal.

Joanna Nealon
New England poet and Co-Editor of
IN Publications in Newton, Massachusetts

ACKNOWLEDGEMENTS

Thanks to the editors of magazines and anthologies where some of these poems first appeared: The Amethyst Review, Blue Skies, Quills, (EX)CITE, The Scarborough Arts Council, The Ontario Poetry Society, The Canadian Authors Association.

Thank you to Joanna Nealon for her editorial insight. Thank you to Anna for her inspiration. Finally, my love and gratitude to Devi and Jarryl, who helped and encouraged me every step of the way.

Contents

Part I

The Hidden Dreamscape

THE WEIGHT OF DREAMS

1

Somewhere on the edge of
Consciousness
Between light and shadow,
Sorrow and joy,
You led me through
A vale of flowers
Towards an empty field
And said:

Here is the heart
I have stolen from you,
And these were your dreams
That now are flowers
No wind
Will ever disturb.

2

Tonight the frogs are singing,
Singing to the stars
From the edge of the pond,
The sound of summer
Stuck in their throats.

How can I show you
The dreams in my heart
When your love is as cold
As the winter wind?

In the deep of night
When the moon sleeps alone
And frogs serenade the stars,
There is no comfort
For the soul that yearns
No comfort for the heart
That dreams.

3

Nothing is ever as it seems
When ghosts invade the empty heart
And fill our eyes with dreams.

Last night the chimes were singing
The way they used to
When the wind
Summoned you back to me.

But nothing is ever as it seems,
Only the cool, unforgiving night
Full of longing
And the shadows of you.

5

4

The crickets are awake tonight,
Their brittle bodies
Reverberating
To fragments of music
Scattered among the fields.

Deep in the canopy
Of wild summer grass,
Their hearts explode
Into choirs of longing.

You are gone
But your presence lingers.

The cool blue dress
You wore on summer days,
The scent of your perfume
Pervading the room,
The shy wildflowers
That graced your open hair.

Pieces of you
Are scattered everywhere.

6

Weightless as water lilies
Floating on a pond,
My heart is a husk
Longing for the rain
That is your love,
Longing for the cloud
That is you.

7

Only in dreams
Does the heart reveal
Its whirlpool of desires.

Lately I find myself
Wanting to drown in you,
To feel your sweet moisture
Warm on my cheek,
To taste the soft flesh of your tongue.

I lie enveloped
In the hush of night,
Recalling the moment
I entered your body,
Wanting only to possess
Your heart.

Daylight, and memory
Dissolves into mist.

My seed lies scattered
On infertile ground,
And I lie awake
Shaken loose from dreams
Wanting only
To feel you again.

The erotic heart never sleeps.

Last night you came to me
With the taste of honey
On your lips
And the scent of spring
In your hair.

And I longed to lose
Myself in you,
To open you
With my tongue
Petal by petal,
Till your love
Leaked down your thighs.

But the light of the sun
Deceived my desire
As your beautiful face
Slowly disappeared,
Leaving me drenched
In the sweat of passion
And the sticky residue of dreams.

9

You come to me
In the gray hour of dawn,
When the guilty get
No sleep.
You come to me
With forgiving lips,
Feeding me dreams
To lift me from despair,

And I lie awake
On the edge of night,
While you peel through the layers
Of my anguished heart,
Dissolving my fears
'Til nothing remains
But the memory
Of our lost love.

10

Last night
I dreamt of a storm
Ripping through the tortured sky,
An animal scream
In the throat of the wind.

I woke in terror
Alone in the dark,
Nerves trembling like leaves
In the cool night air,
My courage,
Gone with you.

11

You were always there
When the rain came
And the wind's claw
Ripped the fragrant rose
From its bed.

You were always there
When the lightning's shaft
Split the elms
And sent crows cawing
Across misty fields.

Now you are
Forever flying away
Like a leaf un-stemmed
By a midnight wind.

Tonight
As the thunder roars
And the sky explodes
In a blinding shimmer,

I will sit here
Tangled in your memory
And hide in vain
From ceaseless rain.

12

No.
I will not let you take
Possession of my heart,
Possession of my soul.

I will not let you
Disturb my dreams
With the halos
Of your hazel eyes.

No
I will be content
Not to breathe life
Into your ghost.

13

You left
When bluebirds stripped
The glowering sky
Of all their summer songs.

You left
When the fields lay wasted
Like a vacant heart
Bereft of any joy.

Now I must live
With this loneliness
And the memory of your face
To keep me warm

Here in this cold
And comfortless room,
While Autumn's last leaves
Are falling.

14

Fall
And everything is falling.
Leaves litter the world,
Their brown and yellow skeletons
Scratching asphalt
Along streets
Bereft of the sound
Of children laughing
And reveling in summer play.

This is the season of letting go,
Of shedding skin,
Of realizations.
I must teach my withering heart
To live again
And leave behind
The memory of your hazel eyes.

Fall
And everything is falling.
Even the gray October sky
Seems darker, closer
Coming down on me,
'Til I feel its weight

Heavy on the chest.

This is the season of gravity
When laws of physics pull apart
Our brave facades
And leave us broken.

But I must let you go
Even as the rose
Discards its petals
And birds strip the sky of song,

I must let you go.

15

There is a photograph in my head
Of terns hovering
Over a lake
As vast and deep
As my dreams.

The lake is a gossamer sponge
Soaking up the sky
With all its permutations
Of shadow and light
While somewhere, your laughter
Shatters the air
And is frozen instantly
Into a memory cell

And then
Frisbees slicing into summer,
A child's balloon
Escaping in the breeze,
Becoming lost, then found,
Then tangled in the trees.

And you, a ghost
Long buried in my heart
Resurrected from the ashes
Of our lost love
With all eternity
Reflected in your eyes.

What was it that you said?

A lifetime can be lived
In a moment of
Bliss.

But your love is a scar
On the surface of my dreams
And immersed in its memory
I am swallowed
Within.

Part II

The Illuminated Dreamscape

THE RAIN KNOWS YOUR NAME

It is raining again.

The rain knows your name.
It sings it to me
All through the night,
Filling me with a longing
I cannot escape
A longing that burns me inside.

The rain calls
From my window,
Its whispery tongue
Licking my ear,
Seducing my senses
With the memory of you
And drowning me in despair.

In these last low hours,
When I miss you most,
When love is a ghost
With your name,
There is no refuge
In the arms of night,
No comfort
In the music of rain.

MEMORY

In this season of rebirth
When the old grow young
And the mind falls prey
To the talons of memory,

I will take your hand
And walk among
The faded landscapes of our past,
When love was fresh
As a springtime rose
And desire
A bloom of the heart.

And we will sit in green fields
Watching cherry blossoms fall away,
And you will hold me close,
Forgiving me
For having dared
To live this dream
Of love.

FORGIVENESS

Winter has come early this year.
The window's tears,
Now icicles,
Hang heavy in the cold outside.

All day I have witnessed
The tenderness of snow,
How it whitens everything
Forgiving the past.

And I wanted to tell you
As you walked out the door
That the permanence of ice
Is misleading.

That I too
Can be as forgiving
And tender
As the snow outside.

THUNDERSTORMS

Deep in the belly
Of the violet bruised sky
Spring clouds rain memories.

The fresh scent of hyacinths
Entwined with the breeze,
Wisps of cherry blossom
Falling gracefully at our feet
As we watched the lightening
Shatter the sky
Into shards of light.

How you shivered
As the thunder's hammer fell,
Your body arching itself
Into mine.
So long ago now
Though I still feel
The warmth of your hands
Holding my heart.

UNCLOTHED

Watching you sleep
As you lie next to me,
Your soft skin
Silvered
By the jealous moon;

No longer the vixen
In the little black dress,
The rebel in blue jeans,
The goddess in a gown;

All your identities
Finally stripped away,
All your facades
Strewn about the floor,
'Til nothing remains
But the underlying woman,
The real you

At last.

STRAWBERRIES AND CREAM

Tonight
You offer your body to me,

Pink nipples dipped
In cool whipped cream,
And your sensual lips
On fire,

And my dry mouth hungers
For the taste of your
Sex
On the tip of my
Tongue,

As slowly, gently
Your garden reveals
Wild strawberries
Ripe

With desire.

BATHROOM MADONNA

Looking for you,
I stumble upon your bathtub,
Your holy retreat
Of soap and bubbles,
Adorned with candles
Alight.

Motionless you lie
With your eyes half closed,
Your spirit soothed
By Gregorian chants
Echoing
From the bathroom radio.

And I feel like
Dropping to my knees
With hands together in reverent prayer,
As you shine and shimmer
Like an apparition
Alight in the incensed air.

HER HANDS

Her hands are not that pretty
Nor are they soft as white rose petals
Cooled by the morning dew,
Their chipped and broken fingernails
Uncared for and unpolished bear
The scars of her impatience
And the saffron stains that show
Her love for nicotine.

Yet her touch is warm and tender
Pouring hope and comfort from
Her understanding palms,
Which hold me in their grip of love
And never lets me fall.

THE LANGUAGE OF OUR SILENCE

Here in the morning light
Between the kettle's hiss
And the crunch of half burnt toast,
The language of our silence
Unfolds between us
In speechless conversations
Made only with our eyes.

We slip into the comfort
Of everyday routines,
As I clear the cups and dishes
And pack away your lunch,
While you ,ever rushing
For the freedom of outside,
Grab your coat and briefcase
Before you kiss
Goodbye.

On this cold November morning
While the trees are weeping leaves,
Even the birds are mute
As I watch you drive
Away.

BLONDE

Today
Coming home from work,
Blondes walked by me
From all directions,
And my bruised heart shuddered
At the sight of gold,

Gold ghosts
That remind me of you.

On this cold October evening
Of yellowed Autumn sky,
Memory has no mercy
When even the trees
Are blonde.

BLUE BUTTERFLIES

Your eyes are blue butterflies
In the morning light,
Fluttering their way
Into my heart.

Caught in the perilous
Gaze of Love,
My soul surrenders
To your blossoming smile,

And I fall in devotion
At your feet,
Wanting only to be
By your side.

PHOENIX

I am getting too old to
Write of love,
And yet
Each time you come to me,
Your mouth, a violet
In full bloom
Your eyes, a sanctuary
To fallen stars,

My heart arises
From the ashes of youth,
Rekindled
With the flame of desire.

PHILOSOPHY CLASS

No sound between us
Except for the momentary
Rush of air
Escaping from your parted lips.

But then
As if struck by a
New realization,
Your head looks up from
Yellowed pages
Singed with tales of old republics,
And you look at me
With a wild fervour,
The evening light scattered
In your Maybelline eyes,
And you whisper

"Plato was right
About the cave and the shadows
And the perception of truth."

While I sit there
Dumbfounded
By the beauty of your smile,
The only truth
I ever believed.

THRUSH SINGING IN THE DEAD OF WINTER

Poor soul,
Betrayed by jealous winds
And blown apart
From the one you love,

I have heard you
Wailing
At break of dawn,
As the bright glow
Of a winter's sun
Thaws not the frost
In your heart.

Sad lover,
Singing in the dark of night
Alone in the shadows
Of leaf stripped trees,

Your music freezes
Inside my ear
And I pray for your death
Because you know
The emptiness
Of unfulfilled dreams.

CARDINAL ON HIGH

I have heard you
Perched on high,
Your voice a harbinger
Of the coming spring.

You are singing,
Singing life back into the trees,
Into the deep brown earth
Where the daffodils yet sleep,

Into the vast expanse
Of barren fields,
Where frozen flowers dream
Of the warm kiss of bees.

I have heard you
In that gray hour before dawn,
Serenading the sun
Still sunk among the clouds;

There, high upon some leafless branch,
Your voice in ecstasy,
Burning, burning your song
Into me.

MOTH

Little moth,
Soft butterfly of night,
Have you come here
In this quiet hour
To take into the air
My vanquished dreams
Above the trembling hands of trees,
Into the blue gray atmosphere?

Dark messenger
Of the spirit world,
What comfort can your presence bring
To a heart so ravaged
By the talons of fear?
O, lift it gently upon your wings
And take it high into the sky
Beyond the grasp of pain,
Beyond the shadows of despair,
Into the blue gray atmosphere.

ON WINTER

Winter
Is a racist.
Covers everyone and everything
In an unforgiving
White.

Stands firm and rigid
Like an old man
Stuck in a lifetime of denial,

Opposing change,
Spring
And the advent
Of colour.

EARLY SPRING

Sprinkles of snow
Are melting into memory,
While birdsong bellows
From tree to tree,
And frost free fields
Come alive
With resurrected flowers.

SPRING SPLENDOR

All night the rain fell
Dissolving snow into nothing more
Than a cold unwanted memory.

Winter's teeth, now dentures,
Have lost their bite,
As songbirds claim the leafless trees
To sing them back to life.

Morning is for miracles,
Soft tender miracles
When all we see are
Myriad flower buds
Birthing into bloom;
When all we smell
Is the earth's bouquet
Awash
In the splendor of Spring.

MAY

All month
I have watched her grow
In the quiet of parks,
Where the robins sing,
The first sweet notes
Of Spring.

No longer a child
In the eyes of Time,
Her beauty dispels all gloom.
Who would have thought
That she could be
So pretty?

April's little sister
In bloom.

GARDEN GREEN

It is quiet and peaceful here
In this green reality
Of plants and trees,
Where the stress and turmoil
Of everyday life
Seems a thousand miles away.

And though I must return
To a world of concrete and steel,
It's easy to lose one's self
In the strange choreography
Of maples caught
In the windswept rapture
Of dance,

Or dream away
While schools of swallows
Sail
The starless sky.

AUTUMN DESCENDS

All day long the cricket's song
Echoed from deep ravines
Stained with hues of autumn.

Summer is spent,
And the last green leaves of the maple
Writhe into a purple sheen,
While the sun sets high
In a kaleidoscope sky,
Where birds fly away
Like a shawl released
Into the winnowing wind.

MAPLE SHEDDING LEAVES IN THE WIND

You were the one that
Caught my eye,
Not the young blondes
Who seem to say,

"Hey you, turn this way
And look at us.
Don't you think
We're slim and beautiful?"

Alone and neglected
At the far edge of the field,
You stand majestic
In your elder years
With all of Autumn
In your auburn hair,
Cascading within the breeze.

MY FATHER AT THE CAR LOT

My father was never a rich man,
Never once got a break
In all his life
Of incessant toil
And financial strain.

But watching him there,
Standing in the car lot
Dreaming of the truck
He knows he'll never own,

Breaks my heart
A thousand times,
As I place my hand
Upon his shoulder

And whisper softly,
"Let's go."

VIOLETS
For my Father

In the crowded Emergency Ward,
The frantic doctors come and go,
Strange masked faces
Calling out to you
From whirling lights and
Flickering beams.

But you are not here.

Lost in the chasm
Of concussive dreams,
You long to return
Down the vista of years
To the violet fields
Of your youth;

While outside
We watch and wait,
Holding silent vigils from our chairs,
As the purple bruise
Above your eye
From cracked cranium crashing
Into the cold ceramic bathroom floor,
Swells softly in the white
Fluorescent light,

Your memory of violets
In bloom.

APOLOGY

You with the smile like
Violets in bloom,
With the touch as tender
As forgiving kisses;

You with the morning
Sun in your hair
And the evening sky
Stretched out in your eyes;

Know that my heart
Still yearns for your love,
Still bleeds out the words,
"I'm sorry."

CHICKADEE

Not much more than an afterthought,
A dark shadow fleeting along
The periphery of memory.
You move, phantom winged,
Among green thickets and scented shrubs
And Spring's wild mane
Of woodland grass.

All but forgotten
Against the splendid array
Of blue plumed jays or
Yellow warblers,
We scarcely notice your
Tiny frame
Except in moments of
Quiet reflection,
When the fields are hushed of
Summer's songs,
And Winter's beauty stills the world,
And we remember

How on those frosty days,
When the others have fled
To warmer climes,
You were the one who stayed behind,

CHICKADEE (cont.)

Brave heart fluttering
Against the cold,
To soothe our minds
With thoughts of spring
And warm our dreams
With summer.

POEM FOR THE CHILDREN OF BESLAN, RUSSIA

In the blue glow of the tv screen,
(The only window into their suffering),
Mothers and fathers are weeping.

Out in the garden
Among the solemn willows,
A robin grieves for her dead chick,
Her plaintive wailing
Caressing my ear
Day after day after day.

In the pink light of evening
Beneath the first few stars of night,
Her tiny heart
Is a fluttering song
Filled with that much love.

When the madness ended
And the smoke cleared
From the classrooms of smoldering ash,
They carried away the dead,
Their broken bodies - light as feathers
In the heat of the midday sun,

While deep in the throat of the garden
Beneath the tender glove of night
For the first time in three long days,
A voice is drowned
In silence.

THE FORTUNE TELLER

Walking through the carnival,
We pass by the old
Gypsy woman,
Her brown face cracked
In the heat of the sun
With the furrowed inscriptions
Of time.

But something about her
Catches your eye,
Draws you to her
Enigmatic smile
That reels you in
Like a fish on the line,
Hooked to the prospect
Of truth.

Five dollars later
She reads your palm,
Arthritic fingers
Tracing the topography
Of your heart
And the contours of your

THE FORTUNE TELLER (cont.)

Hidden dreams.

She tells you your life line
Is strong,
That there are two, no wait,
Three children in the stars
Which promise good fortune
And happiness,
As long as you follow your heart.

She speaks to you
With prophetic tongue,
Her slurred speech soothing
Your eager ears,
As she looks my way
With cursory eyes
And cautions,

"Choose more wisely."

EARLY MORNING POEM

One by one
The lamps of heaven
Extinguish their flames,
Dissolve, and fade away.

This is the moment of truth,
Of bleary eyed dreams
And rasping words
From desert dry tongues.

Like a hopeful parent,
Night gives birth to
Precocious day,
Teaches it to walk
In this first gray hour,
Before letting it go
To stumble forth
Into the bright expanse
Of undiscovered dreams.

So too have I
Fashioned you
In this time of deliverance,
In this hour of promise,
You, who would not wait
For the light of day,
Wanting more than anything
To leave my thoughts
And breathe the air
Of creation.

BODY LANGUAGE

My body speaks to me
With the tongue of Time,

Talks of strength remembered
In aged hands,
Of youth's first kiss
Upon virgin lips,
Of hopes and dreams,
Loves won and lost,
A heart too wild
To understand.

My body speaks to me
Through the wrinkle of years
Furrowed deep into my
Hollowed face,
Through the first gray hairs
That pale my image,
The silent sentinels of time;

For though the mind bleeds itself
Of memory,
Mirror is a voice
Calling out to me,

A keen reminder of yesterday
That the body
Remembers.

OCTOBER SKY

Starlings swarm
To a fluttering heart
Up high, where
Burnt sky
Bleeds the horizon
In cascades of crimson
And gold.

BLACK ICE

You taught me the proper technique,
How to keep my distance
In the blinding snow
And not place faith
In the strength of the brake.

You cautioned
That the ice is always
Smooth and slick
As a used car salesman's tongue.

Remember
Take nothing for granted,
The feel of your hand
On mine.

Now
We hardly ever speak to each other
Except for the occasional hello
Or goodbye,
As somewhere along the way
We've spun out of control,
Lost that centre of gravity

BLACK ICE (cont.)

That held us together
And kept us grounded
In each other's love.

But Father,
Sometimes
On the long journey home,
When the road is iced
With yesterday's tears
And there's no going back
To that point of departure,

My heart still aches
For the touch of your hand
Long after we have both
Let go.

LOVE'S MYTHS

He knew no other way of
Forgetting,
Of absolving himself of
Love's myths.

Years ago
When his heart first felt
The winged boy's dart,
He thought himself a
New Icarus
And dared to brave
Her bright blue eyes
With wildest dreams of love,

(Not knowing she only
Waxed poetic
With small town boys like him).

How like a shooting star
He descended
So deep into his hollow chest
That now he walks
Inside his flesh
With burnt out eyes and
Heart of ash,

Melting out of memory
And myth.

DREAMING FELLINI

No sound between us,
Only the gravity
Of incomplete sentences:
I _____
Do you want...?

Clouds drift
In and out of your eyes.
I'm reaching out,
But you're so far away.

Perhaps
You're dreaming Fellini again,
The black and white
Cobbled streets of Rome
With their tiny cafes
And myriad chapels
Calling out to you,
"La Dolce Vita."

Anywhere but here.

Given half a chance,
I might just bridge
This surreal space
This sense of longing
Inside your heart.
Given half a chance,
I could be your Mastroianni.

OLD GREEN HOUSE

Old green house
Stands on a hill,
Calls out to me
With the tongue of a child
Playing hide and seek
In an upstairs closet,
Lit only by the light
Of memory.

Old green house
Keeps its secrets,
Gathers moss like stone
Watered over by time
That washes away
All remnants of the past.

There's a hole somewhere
In the leaky roof,
A crack in memory
Where water seeps in
And flows down the creaking
Vertebrae of stairs
To purge the dreams
Of bygone years.

Those dreams,
Those years,
These resurrected memories,

All water under the house now.

SALVATION

On the bed
You lie awake
Pure and naked
As the ochre earth
From which your bones emerged.

In this silver hour of twilight,
Violets bloom
Within your eyes,
While your hair spills out
Like golden wheat
Beneath a sea of
Prairie sky.

My darling,
There is no fire left
Within this heart of
Cinder and ash
Within these veins
Whose blood has dried
To hardened quartz.

Time becomes me
In this quest for love,
As I stand before you
With fossilized dreams,
The weight of years
Upon my shoulders,

Seeking salvation
In you.

TALKING IN HER SLEEP

Every night
You talk in your sleep,
Your cryptic tongue
Seducing my ear
With the secrets
Of your heart's desire.

Who is he,
This lover of yours,
The one whose name
Your strawberry lips
Can never quite reveal?

In the tender light of morning,
My dawn is always green,
Knowing you could never
Love me like that,
The way you love him
In your dreams.

About the Poet

Jeevan Bhagwat lives and works in Scarborough, Ontario, Canada.

His work has been published in many literary magazines/websites in Canada and the U.S. including The Amethyst Review, Archaeology, Blue Skies, Quills, and in anthologies by The Ontario Poetry Society and The Canadian Authors Association.

In 2003 and 2005 he was awarded the Monica Ladell Prize for Poetry by the Scarborough Arts Council and in 2011, he won first place in the Conscience Canada Art/New Media contest.

In 1998, his chapbook of poems entitled Night Shadows was published by Plowman Press.